MW01295153

Modern Sāṃkhya:

Ancient Spirituality for the Contemporary Atheist

D. E. OSTO

2016

Palmerston North

New Zealand

©Copyright D. E. Osto

CONTENTS

Introduction

Sāṃkhya is one of the most ancient of India's philosophical traditions and its influence has been widespread in Indian thought for centuries. The *Sāṃkhyakārikā*, composed by Iśvarakṛṣṇa sometime before the mid-sixth century CE, is the one and only source text for what has been called "classical Sāṃkhya." It is a short text of 73 verses outlining the main position of the Hindu philosophy known as the Sāṃkhya School. While there are many later texts (the vast majority not translated or studied) demonstrating the transformations and development of the School throughout the centuries, most contemporary scholars agree that the *Sāṃkhyakārikā* presents the earliest extant source of the classical Sāṃkhyan position.

The central aim of Sāṃkhya, like the other renouncer traditions of India, is to counteract human suffering. To do this, Sāṃkhya proposes a special type of metaphysical dualism, which asserts the absolute distinction between pure consciousness (*puruṣa*) on the one hand, and the phenomenal world (*prakṛti*) on the other. According to Sāṃkhya all psychophysical processes are systemically interconnected in a causally deterministic phenomenal realm, which we can understand as "nature." However, this natural world only becomes manifest when it reacts to being "witnessed" by individual nodes of pure consciousness. Each node represents a pure transcendental subject, which is a completely passive observer or witness to the phenomenal world. In this regard, while the natural world is considered ontologically real, it manifests in a particularly distinctive way for each node of consciousness. Thus Sāṃkhya may be viewed as asserting a special type of philosophical "perspectivism." According to Sāṃkhya, liberation is attained

3

through the practice of discriminating all the various processes of the psychophysical entity and disassociating from them as either "me" or "mine." Once all possible phenomena in the field of consciousness are recognized as not consciousness, nature returns to its unmanifest state and the transcendental subject resides isolated (*kaivalya*) in its own nature; thus liberation from suffering has been obtained.

Modern Sāṃkhya

The ancient philosophy of Sāṃkhya can be applied to modern life in a number of valuable ways. Rather than becoming overly concerned with the metaphysics of the system, Sāṃkhya can be seen as a psychological tool to overcome suffering. Through rigorous philosophical and psychological analysis, a person can learn to detach or disassociate from the psychophysical entity, and realize witness consciousness or what I refer to as the transcendental subject.

I have subtitled this work "Ancient Spirituality for the Contemporary Atheist" because with little modification Sāṃkhya can be adapted to modern life and a contemporary atheistic worldview. Classical Sāṃkhya postulates no God, supreme being, or creator of the universe. The fact of the material world is taken as a given – no creator needed. However, Sāṃkhya is a form of spirituality in the sense that it recognizes the possibility of transcendence. Each of us has the potential to rise above our human condition and attain a state or condition beyond the limitations of our individuality, psychology, physical body, social conditioning, historical context, and even the spacetime continuum we find ourselves in. Thus Sāṃkhya shows us that there is not a necessary dichotomy between atheism and spirituality. Moreover, its understanding of the human condition, the self, and the universe provide us with profound psychological insights that may be utilized for better living in this world.

EXERCISE 1: Beyond the Material Plane

YOU are not your bank account; you are not old or young, fat or skinny, good-looking or ugly, tall or short. You are not your personality, your personal history, your wants, desires, hopes, dreams, fantasies, or memories. The psychophysical entity you think you are is not you. It is a part of nature. All of it – bones, blood, organs, brain, thoughts, memories, and personality – is linked inexorably to the laws of physics, cause and effect, and is part of an interconnected web of conditioning by the society, culture and environment in which it is located. But none of this is YOU.

So what are YOU? YOU are the WITNESS. You are a node of pure consciousness; the transcendental subject that is the "enjoyer" of all phenomena. Without this source consciousness there would be no experience at all. All experience is experience from a particular point of view. That point is you. And as the ancient texts assert, "the eye cannot see itself." In this case, it is "the 'I' cannot see itself." But this "I" is not your ego; your ego is merely a construct, and it also is a part of the world of nature. You as witness are and always have been free; you have never been bound by any suffering, sadness, depression, or loss.

Ancient Indian Origins of Sāṃkhya

Sāṃkhya's beginnings go back to ancient India perhaps as early as 800 BCE. Between 800 and 400 BCE, profound changes took place in the religious landscape of India. A new religious and philosophical outlook arose collectively known as the "renouncer traditions." These new religious movements shared certain presuppositions about who we are and what the world is like. Prior to this, Vedic religion was primarily concerned with correct ritual performance, which would lead to beneficial this-worldly results (such as sons, long life, good crops, cattle, etc.). Here, I outline some of the most fundamental ideas that emerged in this new religious context.

One central idea of the systems is karma. Karma (*karman* in Sanskrit) is the notion that there is a cause and effect relation between one's intentional actions and the results of those actions. In other words, actions possess a certain potency that leads to positive or negative results in the future. An important corollary to this belief is the idea that karma not only affects this life, but past and future lives as well. Not only are we born as human beings, but we may also be reborn as animals, in heavens, or hells. We can even come back as spirits or ghosts! There is no beginning to this process, so each person has had countless past lives as various beings in different worlds and will continue to be reborn or reincarnated until the cycle is stopped. One's karma is thought to determine not only what kind of world one will be reborn in, but also such things as one's gender, social status, physical appearance and wealth. Good karma will lead to a happy rebirth as a human or god; whereas bad karma will lead to unfortunate rebirth in hell, or as an animal or ghost. There is obviously an ethical or moral dimension to the notion of what constitutes good or bad karma; however, the details of what exactly leads to negative or positive results, and the extent or severity of karmic retribution was always subject to debate. Nevertheless, it was widely accepted by the renouncers that harming other living beings was a cause of serious karmic demerit. Thus, nonviolence (*ahiṃsa*) became a vital component to a renouncer's religious practice.

Important corollary beliefs to karma and rebirth are "*saṃsāra*" and "*mokṣa*." Saṃsāra is the name given to the endless cycle of reincarnation. Since they believed saṃsāra is primarily characterized by impermanence and suffering, the renouncers maintained that life as ordinarily lived is ultimately unsatisfactory.

Thus the goal becomes to escape the painful cycle of rebirth by attaining liberation (*mokṣa*). The renouncer traditions conceived of *mokṣa* as a permanent state or freedom from the cycle of *saṃsāra*. The specifics of this state and the means by which it is attained varies from school to school, but all the renouncers believed that in order to escape one needed to renounce or "drop out" of the social world altogether by giving up one's spouse, children, sexuality, wealth and social status. This was often conceived of as a spiritual death whereby the individual "dies" to the social world in order to begin the life of a wandering ascetic in search of release. This transformation often included joining a fraternity of renouncers (or more rarely a sorority, if the renouncer were a woman), who were dependent upon a lay following for such material support as food and clothing. However, dropping out of society was not considered sufficient in and of itself for liberation. During countless previous lives an individual would have accumulated karma that would inevitably lead to rebirth unless it was somehow "burned off." Thus enters asceticism, the practice of physical and mental austerities such as fasting and exposing oneself to extremes of heat and cold in order to remove pre-existing negative karma.

Renunciation of society and asceticism were often seen as only the preconditions for escape; to permanently cut off future rebirths, something else was required. That something else was a special type of knowledge, or intuitive insight into the nature of reality, often referred to in Sanskrit as *jñāna* (from the Sanskrit root *jñā-*, meaning "to know;" cognate through the Greek, to English "gnosis"). The overwhelming conclusion of the renouncers is that sentient beings are ultimately inactive, eternal, unchanging souls (variously called *ātman, jīva, puruṣa*), which have somehow become confused or entangled in the saṃsāric process of activity, change and suffering. Thus the goal of liberation becomes one of attaining a direct intuitive realization of one's true self as inactive, eternal, and unchanging. Meditation was believed to be the method by which such a realization is made possible. Here we see a fusion between philosophy and salvation: the Indian philosophical systems, because they seek to know the true nature of the self and its relation to reality in order to achieve liberation, are always about spiritual transcendence.

Thus, according to these philosophies, an individual can achieve freedom from this state of bondage by overcoming ignorance. Through various types of ethical development, renunciation, contemplation and meditation, the individual can attain the necessary knowledge concerning the fundamental nature of reality and thereby achieve a permanent state of freedom. The different schools possess different interpretations of how this is done and what it means, but all agree that it is the highest goal and entails freedom from the results of karma.

Sāṃkhya and Classical Yoga

Students of classical Yoga as found in Patañjali's *Yoga Sūtra* will notice strong similarities between Sāṃkhya and Patañjali's Yoga. Both systems accept the fundamental duality between consciousness and the world. And both aim for the complete isolation of the self from the world. In the past some commentators have viewed the two schools as different aspects of the same school such that Sāṃkhya provides the metaphysics and classical Yoga outlines the practice necessary to attain liberation. I personally view Sāṃkhya and Yoga as independent systems that happen to share certain philosophical assumptions about the world and the self, but employ different methods for attaining liberation. Whereas Yoga places great emphasis on concentration as the culmination of a progressive eight-stage path (*aṣṭāṅga*), Sāṃkhya employs analytical investigation and discrimination between what is pure consciousness and what is the world, in order to attain ultimate release. Another important

8

difference is that classical Yoga believes in the existence of "the Lord" or a God, who can act as an object of devotion. As mentioned above, Īśvarakṛṣṇa's Sāṃkhya philosophy is an atheistic path to liberation.

Sāṃkhya and Buddhism

With the development of the renouncer traditions a number of new religious philosophies arose both within orthodox Hinduism and outside of it. Some of the important Hindu schools are classical Sāṃkhya, Patañjali's Yoga, and later the "nondual" or Advaita Vedānta. The most important non-Hindu school to develop in this period is Buddhism. Like the other renouncers, Buddha accepted the ideas of karma, rebirth and liberation (which Buddhists call "nirvana"). He also accepted the notion that the cycle of rebirth is painful, and that the ultimate goal of existence is to transcend this cycle. Unlike the other traditions, Buddha rejected the idea that there is any permanent self or soul (this is known as the doctrine of "no-self"). However, there are strong similarities between classical Sāṃkhya and the early Buddhist teachings, which will become obvious to any reader with some prior knowledge of Buddhism.

Although both Sāṃkhya and Buddhism emerged from the same historical context in ancient India and share a number of important features characteristic of the renouncer traditions, the two have followed substantially different paths since. Buddhism eventually travelled beyond India and spread throughout all of Asia, and in the modern period has undergone profound changes during its transmission to the West. Sāṃkhya, on the other hand, while exerting a profound influence on Indian thought throughout the centuries, never took root beyond India, and has all but become extinct as an independent religious philosophy in the modern period.

9

One of the most profound changes to occur to Buddhism in its encounter with modernity has been termed "psychologization." This is the process whereby Buddhism is viewed as psychology and its mythological and traditional aspects are either downplayed or ignored. This has in turn led to the "Buddhicization" of psychology, whereby growing numbers of psychologists in the West use Buddhist concepts and techniques for therapeutic reasons. We see this most clearly in the "mindfulness" craze that has entered mainstream psychology in the United States. Thus a detraditionalized, psychologized Buddhism is now firmly entrenched within the American medical and psychotherapeutic communities. Another aspect of this new Buddhism is the downplaying or complete ignoring of the world-renouncing aspects of Buddhism, in favor of the "this-worldly" benefits of Buddhism.

The above comments are not meant as a criticism of modern Buddhism or how it is used by some people in the contemporary world. Rather it is to point out that religions and religious philosophies are constantly undergoing changes and transformations in order to adapt to the needs of people. These days renouncing the world to become a wandering ascetic is not a viable option for most people living in modern, industrialized societies. Moreover, few people would choose to give up all their worldly possessions, emotional attachments, erotic relationships, and family ties to pursue a transcendent state beyond space, time, decay and death. However, what many people today want as much as the ancient Indian renouncers is to live a life free from suffering, and attain some type of lasting happiness.

Aim of the Book

This book proposes a modernization of the ancient classical Sāṃkhya system in order to modernize it like certain contemporary types of Buddhism. To do this, we can investigate the *Sāṃkhyakārikā* of Īśvarakṛṣṇa to uncover its important psychological insights concerning our human condition and the means to transcend it. Thus I recommend a psychologization of Sāṃkhya not unlike modern Buddhism. In many ways, Sāṃkhyan spirituality is well suited to the modern atheist – it does not include worship of a supreme deity, belief in infallible sacred scripture, following an ecclesiastical hierarchy, demand for blind faith, the practice of empty ritualism and meaningless ceremony, or adherence to some New Age wooly-eyed optimism; however, it does aim at spiritual transcendence through adherence to a new philosophical outlook based on individual self-enquiry, analytical discrimination, and discerning the fundamental facts concerning our human condition.

I have studied Asian religious philosophies and practiced various meditation techniques for over thirty years. Currently, I teach Asian studies and Asian philosophies at Massey University in New Zealand. In addition to my academic studies and personal meditation practice, during the last several years I have also taught mindfulness meditation (see my website www.douglasosto.com for more details). Although most of my training and academic writing have been on Buddhism, for over a decade I have studied Sāṃkhya philosophy. During this time, I have been continually amazed by the intuitive strength of some of Sāṃkhya's fundamental notions, and impressed by the strong parallels that exist between Sāṃkhya and Buddhism. However, Sāṃkhya is not merely Buddhism by another name, but makes strong arguments about the nature of experience that are decidedly different from Buddhism. Moreover, I feel that some aspects of Sāṃkhya actually resonate better with certain features of modern, Western thought.

Although Sāṃkhya possesses an extensive collection of philosophical writings, Īśvarakṛṣṇa in his *Sāṃkhyakārikā* succinctly annunciates the fundamental ideas of the classical system in a mere 73 verses. Thus by focusing on this short text, one can, I believe, reconstruct and reinterpret the philosophy for utilization in the contemporary world. Much of my understanding of Sāṃkhya philosophy has been strongly influenced by Gerald James Larson, who unquestionably is the foremost scholar of the system in the contemporary English speaking world. His *Classical Sāṃkhya: An Interpretation of its History and Meaning* (Second Revised Edition, 1979) offers profound insights into the system. However, I have my own views on the system, and how it might be used for practical psychological purposes by people today. And as far as I know, no one has ever attempted to reconstruct classical Sāṃkhya to be utilized as a contemporary spiritual path.

Since the goal of this book is to present "Modern Sāṃkhya" as a contemporary and practical path toward transcending personal suffering, I have eschewed the use of extensive referencing, bibliography and index in favor of a more direct writing style. Because the goal is practical philosophy, I have also included throughout the book textboxes with exercises to aid in the internalization of the Sāṃkhyan philosophical outlook. One should view these exercises as "meditations" meant to focus and train the mind to perceive the world in a way conducive to the Sāṃkhyan goal of transcendence. I also include in Chapter III, my own complete translation of the *Sāṃkhyakārikā*, so that the interested reader may gain a better understanding of the classical system in a manner closer to that presented by Īśvarakṛṣṇa, the master himself. Since this book has been written as a practical guidebook for activating Sāṃkhya philosophy, the reader should feel free to use whatever resonates with him or her, and to disregard the rest.

I. The Self and the World

Īśvarakṛṣṇa (or "Īśvara" for short) begins the *Sāṃkhyakārikā* (SK) with the observation that we suffer, and therefore desire to be free from it (*Sāṃkhyakārikā*, verse 1; or SK1). This seems to be intuitively true – no one likes to suffer. Even the masochist cries out in pain when he falls down the stairs and breaks his leg. And we suffer from all kinds of things – physical pain, psychological pain, pain inflicted on us by others, and pain from just being a finite being in a material world. There are natural disasters, plagues, famines, floods, car crashes, plane crashes, earthquakes, and tsunamis. We get sick; get cancer, heart disease, and diabetes. We grow old and we die. These are the cold hard facts of our existence. To deny them is to deny the human condition. However, rather than giving in to despair, Īśvara believes that the truth can set us free. So he searches for a solution to this most fundamental problem.

At first he considers "perceptible means" – what we would call "natural remedies" to suffering – such as medicines, therapy, healthy living, etc. But he rejects these because such solutions are not final; they are only temporary fixes to a deeper problem (SK1). Likewise, he rejects all scriptures and revealed truths, because he sees these as also fallible and not guaranteeing permanent release from suffering (SK2). Then he tells his reader his solution, which he says is superior to both: discriminative knowledge (*vijñāna*) of the "manifest" (*vyakta*), the "unmanifest" (*avyakta*) and the "knower" (*jña*) (SK2). Thus in the first two verses, Īśvara spells out the fundamental problem with the human condition (suffering), and the solution to this problem (acquiring a special type of knowledge concerning what is manifest, what is unmanifest, and the one who knows).

The next 66 verses explain how this is done. Īśvara outlines his program using technical terminology that is highly specialized for the philosophical debates and discussions Sāṃkhyans engaged with other philosophers for generations. In explaining it here, I reduce the Sanskrit jargon to a minimum in order to convey Īśvara's message as directly as I can to the modern English-speaking person. Basically, Īśvara is concerned with three fundamental questions:

1. "What is the true nature of the world?"
2. "What is our true nature as human beings?"
3. "How can we distinguish the fundamental difference between the two?"

According to Īśvara, if we can correctly answer these questions, in other words, if we can know the true nature of reality, this knowledge has the power to free us permanently from suffering.

Means of knowledge

Let us look first at the world. How do we know anything about the world we live in? Like the other Indian philosophers, Īśvara asserts we gain knowledge of the world through two primary means: perception and inference. We know things about the world because we have sense organs like eyes, ears, nose, skin, and tongue with which we contact the world and receive information. For Indian thinkers, the mind was also seen as another "organ" of sense that perceives thoughts. So through these six senses, we gain knowledge about the world. We also gain knowledge through inference and reliable authority. For instance, if we see smoke on the hill, we can infer there is a fire. Another practical example is our knowledge about the existence of other minds. We have no direct access to others' minds, but we can infer they have them from the way they are acting. We could be wrong – perhaps they are actually mindless robots, which only appear to have minds. Nonetheless, we need to make inferences about the world based on our perceptions in order to act. However, we know (or at least think we know) a lot more about the world than from just using our perception and inference. Science for instance tells us that the circumference of the world is about 25,000 miles, the distance to the sun is around 93 million miles, and our galaxy is approximately 100,000 light years across – facts we take on reliable authority. Regularly in our lives we accept the views, opinions and beliefs of authority figures such as academics, doctors, lawyers and scientists. Again, they could be wrong, but it would be impossible to function in the world if we didn't accept some truths based on reliable authority.

When we seriously investigate the world through our senses, we realize how subjective experience is. For example, my eye sight and hearing are not particularly good. Glasses help my vision, but I haven't done anything about my hearing yet. Because of this a younger person with better vision and hearing will experience things I simply don't have access to. Some people are blind or deaf, and have never seen colors or heard music. Also, animals experience the world very differently based on different sense organs. A dog's sense of smell is ten thousand times greater than a human's. This opens whole domains of smell to dogs that we have no direct knowledge of. Moreover, we each have private access to our emotions, thoughts, memories, and sensations that others do not. My experience of a sunny spring morning might be radically different from yours given our different histories, emotional states, sense organs, and chemical activity in our brains. Thus I actually live in the world *as it manifests to me*; in other words, I live in my own version of the world. Given the radically subjective nature of experience, we could go so far as saying that each living thing inhabits the center of its own universe. Thus in some sense we are each alone in our own world.

This raises an important philosophical question: Since I only have direct access to my own experience, am I the only being that actually exists? This view that I am the only being that exists is known in philosophy as "solipsism." However, this seems to go against common sense. It really feels like there are other people in the world besides me. You'll be happy to know that Sāṃkhya rejects solipsism, in favor of what I call "perspectivism." This is because, although we have no direct perception of other conscious beings, we can infer their existence from our perceptions of their physical actions in the material world.

The World

In the *Sāṃkhyakārikā*, Īśvara calls the world "*prakṛti*." Prakṛti literally means "making or placing before, or at first." It is a term used to indicate the original or natural form or condition of anything; its original or primary substance. According to the SK, prakṛti is the first principle, the root cause, out of which the world of our experience evolves (SK2–3). Common definitions of prakṛti by contemporary scholars are "matter," "materiality" or "nature." Here I will often just use "the world" as a translation of prakṛti. According to Īśvara, the world exists in two basic forms: unmanifest (or invisible), and manifest (or visible). Unmanifested prakṛti is uncaused, infinite, pervasive, inactive, singular, and unconscious (SK10). Its imperceptibility is due to its subtle nature, but it exists and may be inferred from the objects around us (SK8). Manifest prakṛti is caused, impermanent, non-pervasive, active, plural, supported, originated, composite, and dependent (SK10). So what does this mean?

The world as each of us experiences it is "manifest prakṛti." The way that it appears to every sentient being is a particular manifestation of the unmanifest prakṛti. This is why the manifest, or visible prakṛti is caused, finite, and plural. My world is caused by my experience of it; this experience is finite; and because there are many beings (countless), who are each subjectively experiencing their own versions of the world, the manifest worlds are many – one for each being in fact. These manifest worlds are made of many parts (composite), and are supported and dependent, because they depend on some subjective consciousness to experience them for their existence. However, each of these worlds shares a common world, which is the unmanifest, or invisible prakṛti. This is "The World" as pure potential, pure energy, or pure possibility, prior to its observation by a subjective consciousness. It is the "World as It Is," in itself, in its own nature, and not as experienced. According to Sāṃkhya, the world in itself cannot be perceived, but we can infer its existence from our experience of the manifest worlds we find ourselves in. Moreover, Īśvara claims that it is the "First Cause" of all the limitless worlds and therefore has no cause, or limit. Thus sometimes Īśvara calls prakṛti "the originator" (*pradhāna*). Because it only acts when observed and made manifest, the unmanifest world is said to be without activity, or division or consciousness. Thus we each inhabit our own world, which nevertheless overlaps with other worlds and shares with them all a common larger, imperceptible world. We can understand this as a type of philosophical perspectivism, in the sense that "reality" is what appears to each of us from our own perspective.

MANY SELVES EACH EXPERIENCING THEIR OWN VERSION OF THE UNMANIFEST WORLD

An analogy I like to use with my students to explain the difference between manifest and unmanifest prakṛti might be handy for you to conceptualize the difference. Imagine an infinitely vast warehouse filled with countless packages, boxes, furniture, etc., which is in complete darkness. However, within this warehouse people wander around each carrying their* own flashlight, which they use to see what's immediately around them. Now each person can only see the part of the warehouse that their flashlight shines on, but because people are occupying the same warehouse, there are overlaps. In this way, some people can see the same things, and so share the same experiences of them. In this analogy, the warehouse is unmanifest prakṛti, and the portions of the warehouse illuminated by the individual flashlights are manifest prakṛti.

---

* Here, and from now on, I use the (possibly less correct) plural "their" or "they" as an inclusive pronoun for both male and female.

The Self

We now need to examine in more detail who these subjective conscious beings are that are experiencing the world each from their own point of view. This strikes at the heart of a perennial philosophical question asked repeatedly throughout human history: "Who am I?" Or in other words, "What is the nature of the self?" Sāṃkhya's answer to this question is both radical and profound; and according to Īśvara, holds the key to ultimate freedom.

The *Sāṃkhyakārikā* calls the true self *"puruṣa."* The word puruṣa in Sanskrit literally means "man" or "person," and is the term used in the ancient Hindu myth of the "cosmic person" who was ritually dismembered resulting in the four main Hindu classes emerging from his body parts. However, in the SK, puruṣa has a specific, technical and philosophical meaning. Īśvara tells us that "puruṣa is neither a producer nor produced" (SK3) and that although the puruṣa is not manifest in experience, it is conscious (SK11). In fact, in the Sāṃkhya system puruṣa is the only thing that is conscious; and more so, it is consciousness itself. The fact that sentient beings are sentient, that is, that they have awareness, is because every being possesses a puruṣa, or node of pure consciousness, which functions as the center of the manifest world as it appears to them. Īśvara tells us that puruṣas are not manifest, which means that they never appear as an object of awareness, because they are awareness itself. They are transcendent subjects residing outside of the material world. That they are neither a producer nor are produced means that puruṣas are not created by anything, nor do they create anything. In fact, according to Sāṃkhya, puruṣas don't do anything (SK19)! They are said to be completely passive witnesses to the manifest world of objects, which emerges out of puruṣa's contact with unmanifest world (prakṛti).

Contemporary scholars commonly translate puruṣa as "self," "soul" or "spirit." Gerald Larson offers more technical translations such as "the principle of consciousness," "pure consciousness," "contentless consciousness," or "simply the fact of individual, impersonal consciousness." Here I use "self" or "true self," "pure consciousness," "nodes of consciousness," or the "transcendent subject" to translate puruṣa. "Self" is probably the simplest translation as long as we understand the special meaning this has within Sāṃkhya philosophy.

A good way to understand the Sāṃkhya view of the self is to imagine you are sitting in a theater watching a movie that you become completely engrossed in – so much so that at a certain point you believe you are actually the main character and everything that is happening to that character is actually happening to you. So if you were watching the *Matrix*, you would think that everything Neo did or said, you were doing or saying. Or if you were watching the original *Star Wars*, everything that was happening to Luke Skywalker, was happening to you. You would think, "I am Luke Skywalker," "This is my life," etc. When in actual fact, you are simply a passive witness to the movie.

When we investigate the Sāṃkhya of the SK, it is important to remember that Īśvara is primarily concerned with the world as we subjectively experience it. Sāṃkhya philosophers tackle the most fundamental problem of our human condition: "Why do we suffer?" They believe that to answer this problem one must first analyze experience into all of its component parts, and understand how these parts work together. Once this is done, one could search within experience for a solution to the problem. In their investigations these philosophers decided that all of experience could be divided into two fundamental principles: the world (prakṛti), and a consciousness that experiences the world (puruṣa). If there were no world, there could be no experience. Likewise, if there were no

22

conscious identity to experience the world, there would be no experience. In other words, in order for there to be something, rather than nothing, there must be both a world (as object) and consciousness (as subject). Moreover, the consciousness that experiences the world cannot be the same thing as the world, since its fundamental characteristic (to be conscious) is different from the unconscious world of objects. Also, since we all experience the world differently from our own subjective point of view, Sāṃkhyans assert that there must be many different nodes of awareness, each functioning as the center of its own subjective (manifest) world (SK18). However, since we share experiences with other seemingly sentient beings, all of our subjective fields of experience must share some common source – a single unmanifest world.

David Chalmers, one of the leading contemporary philosophers of mind, has said that understanding the nature of consciousness is "the hard problem" for philosophy of mind. This is because even with current science and technology, we still cannot give an adequate account of how we are able to have a subjective experience of the world. In other words, despite huge advances in biochemistry and brain scanning technologies, we still cannot understand how brain states translate into the subjective experiences of say physical pain, the color red, the taste of ice cream, or being in love. Thus there is a gap between our knowledge of the world through physics, biology and chemistry, and our subjective or phenomenological experience of the world. In modern Western thought, this gap goes back to the philosopher Descartes' dualism between mind and matter. Although dualist like Descartes, Sāṃkhya proposes a different type of dualism: one between consciousness and matter.

In Sāṃkhya's division, everything that can ever be experienced in the phenomenal world is part of matter (prakṛti). This includes all of our own private experiences of our thoughts, feelings,

23

emotions and memories. In other words, all of our personal psychology, including our ordinary sense of self or ego, is considered part of the material world. However, in order for any of these experiences to emerge out of the unmanifest world, they need to be witnessed by a conscious entity. The interaction or connection of a particular node of consciousness with matter leads to the evolution or emergence of the phenomenal world of subjective experience (SK20).

Evolution

Although we only have direct experience of our subjective worlds, Sāṃkhya believes there must be a "real world out there,'" which is the cause of our experience. By inference from our experience of causality in the phenomenal world, Sāṃkhyan thinkers postulate an imperceptible First Cause to our visible, subjective worlds. This First Cause is itself uncaused, and the phenomenal worlds that emerge from it are the result of its interaction or association with different nodes of pure consciousness. Although it is invisible and infinite, unmanifest prakṛti is made up of three principle constituents, aspects or elements (guṇa). Like the ancient Chinese theory of yin and yang, which views the natural world as emerging from two fundamental principles, Sāṃkhyans believe that the world of nature can be reduced to the three aspects they call sattva, rajas and tamas. These have different qualities and manifest in different ways at the psychological and gross material levels.

Sattva is purity, luminosity, reflection, buoyancy, and pleasure; rajas is energy, activity, stimulation, motion, passion, and pain; tamas is solidity, heaviness, dullness darkness, inertia, and limitation (SK11-13). These three exist in a perfect state of equilibrium within unmanifest prakṛti; however, when the Invisible World contacts a node of subjective awareness, the three aspects fall out of perfect balance and the visible world of phenomena emerges. We can imagine this as a type of chemical reaction between a node of pure consciousness and the material world. Everything that subsequently evolves from this reaction will consist of different portions or ratios of the three aspects. Thus Sāṃkhyans maintain that all causality is the result of the disequilibrium and continued transformations of the three aspects, which have existed eternally and uncaused within primordial nature.

Like yin and yang in Chinese thought, the guṇas are believed to interact in dynamic tension with each other – sometimes one quality predominates over the others. Thus fire is mainly rajas; a rock is mostly tamas; water is very sattvic. Indian medicine (Ayurveda) was heavily influenced by the theory of guṇas and analyzes sickness and health based on it. Thus someone with a high fever has an excess of rajas; a depressed person possesses too much tamas; someone with clarity of thought possesses a sattvic intellect, etc. Just as yin is portrayed by the color black and yang by the color white in Chinese thought, we can imagine sattva as white, rajas as red and tamas as black (see diagram).

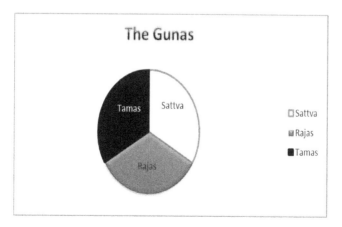

Īśvara presents the transformation of the invisible world in response to a point of subjectivity as an evolution from the most subtle psychological principles to the most gross and material ones. Remember the SK is primarily concerned with the existential or subjective experience of the world – The World as such is imperceptibly subtle and can only be inferred from the unbalancing of the three guṇas. The first principle to evolve out of the Invisible World is called *buddhi*, and sometimes *mahat*, "the Great One." Īśvara states that it is characterized by the power of apprehension (SK23). Because the concept of buddhi overlaps with both the concepts of "will" and "intellect" in English, I will translate it here with "intellect-will," or just leave it untranslated as "buddhi." As the first creation of prakṛti, buddhi is the most basic, subtle, refined object of consciousness we can ever possess. I could way to conceptualize buddhi is to think of an infant when she is first learning about her hands. At first her hands flail around like snakes. After several months, she begins to gain conscious control over them and can use them to grab things, which she immediately puts in her mouth. Here we witness the power of apprehension (she recognizes that her hands are separate things) and will (that she can make them do things, such as grab and pick up other objects in her environment). These represent the activation of her intellect-will.

The next principle to evolve from the intellect-will is the ego (*ahaṃkāra*) (SK22). Ahaṃkāra literally means in Sanskrit the "I-maker." In other words, this is the principle that generates our sense of self as separate from our environment. Again we can see this with small children. Before a sense of separate self emerges, a little one's will is already active. Learning to use their hands and feet, to grab, to crawl, to climb, to vocalize, children develop a sense of self, what Īśvara calls the "self-conceit" (*abhimāna*) (SK24). When we think such things as, "I am going to the store," "I will eat dinner," "I feel sad," the "I" we are referring to is our ego, or constructed sense of self. SK24 states that from the ego evolves the "group of eleven"

26

and the "five subtle elements." The eleven are the mind, the five sense capacities (hearing, feeling, seeing, tasting, and smelling), and the five action capacities (speaking, grasping, walking, excreting, and orgasm), which make up the subjective modes of materiality. The five subtle elements are sound, touch, form, taste, and smell. From these emerge the five gross elements of space, wind, fire, water and earth. The subtle and gross elements together constitute the objective modes of materiality (see diagram).

25 Principles (*tattvas*) of Sāṃkhya

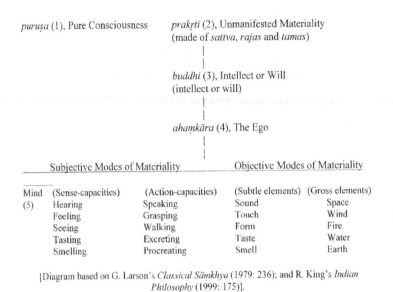

puruṣa (1), Pure Consciousness   *prakṛti* (2), Unmanifested Materiality
(made of *sattva, rajas* and *tamas*)

buddhi (3), Intellect or Will
(intellect or will)

ahaṃkāra (4), The Ego

Subjective Modes of Materiality			Objective Modes of Materiality	
Mind	(Sense-capacities)	(Action-capacities)	(Subtle elements)	(Gross elements)
(5)	Hearing	Speaking	Sound	Space
	Feeling	Grasping	Touch	Wind
	Seeing	Walking	Form	Fire
	Tasting	Excreting	Taste	Water
	Smelling	Procreating	Smell	Earth

[Diagram based on G. Larson's *Classical Sāṃkhya* (1979: 236); and R. King's *Indian Philosophy* (1999: 175)].

As mentioned above, Īśvara views the mind (*manas*) as another organ of sense (SK27). Just as the eyes see visual objects, the mind perceives mental objects such as thoughts, memories and images. The subjective modes and objective modes of materiality consist of everything else that appears in the phenomenal world. When added all together Sāṃkhya's classification results in 25 principles. This list is meant to provide an exhaustive account of reality. Principles 1 and 2 are imperceptible as objects of consciousness. Principles 3-25 consist of everything that can be experienced by a witnessing consciousness, and result from transformations of the three aspects, which begins as a result of disequilibrium among the guṇas through their contact with a consciousness (puruṣa). In other words, the connection of puruṣa and prakṛti leads to the creation of the phenomenal world of experience.

In philosophical terms we may understand Sāṃkhya to be a form of ontological dualism. The system postulates an absolute distinction between the self and the world. Neither is reducible to the other, and both are necessary for experience to occur. When the light of consciousness shines upon the Invisible World, the manifest world appears. With the creation of the subjective world of experience a confusion takes place between the conscious subject and the unconscious field of experience, so that the passive witness (the node of pure consciousness) appears to experience activity and transformation, and aspects of unconscious matter (such as the intellect-will, ego and mind) appear to possess consciousness (SK20). Because of this confusion the disinterested witness is subject to decay and death (SK55). For Sāṃkhya this is why we suffer; we do not know who we really are, and because of this we identify with the world of experience and suffer the vicissitudes of finite existence. With true knowledge of reality we are able to transcend completely the limitations of finite existence.

Exercise 4: Just Watching

Sit in a quiet place, with your spine straight and your hands resting on your thighs or folded in your lap. Gently close your eyes. Begin by taking a few deep breaths, and then breathe naturally. Follow the sensation of your breath as it goes in and out, in and out. Now notice the sensations as they occur in the body; be aware of feelings, emotions, and thoughts as they come and go. Notice sounds in the room, the temperature of the air and the feel of your clothes against your skin. Notice any stiffness, aches or tensions in your muscles. While doing this simply be mindful of what is happening in the present moment without identifying with anything as "me" or "mine."

Now turn your attention to the witness. Who is observing all of these sensations, emotions, feelings, thoughts and perceptions? Is this awareness part of the phenomena or something separate? Can you be the watcher and simply observe what is happening without involvement in the psychological and physiological processes happening in and around the mind and body you have up until now identified with? Realize the mind-body complex is part of the natural world of causality, space, time and change.

Could the conscious witness of it all be something else entirely?
****

II. Transcendence

In the previous section, we saw how Sāṃkhya proposes a radical dualism between consciousness and the world, puruṣa and prakṛti. Each of us as an individual lives in our own version of reality generated from the contact of our true self with the external world. For Sāṃkhya this true self has been pared down to the mere fact of consciousness, a node of pure subjectivity, which allows experience to happen through its proximity to the material world. Our bodies, and even our thoughts, feelings, emotions, memories, plans, hopes, dreams, desires, fantasies, sensations, and all experiences belong to the material world of process, change, sickness, old age and death. But we are not part of this. In truth, we are passive witnesses to this process, forever unchanging, infinite, and eternal sparks of consciousness. However, for some reason we have identified with a part of material world as "me" and "mine," which leads to involvement with this world characterized by impermanence and suffering.

For classical Sāṃkhya this misidentification with the material process has gone on for each individual node of consciousness for countless lifetimes and will continue forever unless specific measures are taken to stop it. This is possible because Sāṃkhya postulates the existence of a "subtle body" (*liṅga*) that survives physical death. This subtle body Īśvara calls "the thirteenfold instrument" because it consists of thirteen principles (intellect-will, ego, mind, the five sense capacities, and the five action capacities). It is thought to transmigrate carrying a being's karma from one lifetime to the next through the force of the dispositions (*bhāva*). The dispositions reside within the "internal organ" (antaḥkaraṇa) made up of the buddhi, ego and mind; more specifically they are said to be qualities of the intellect-will (SK23).

According to Īśvara, the buddhi has four pure or sattvic dispositions and four dark or tamasic dispositions (SK23). The pure dispositions are: knowledge, virtue, dispassion, and power; the dark dispositions are the opposites of these: ignorance, vice, passion, and impotence. Īśvara states that through virtue one acquires good karma and moves up the chain of beings to pleasant realms of rebirth; and through vice one descends into the lower, painful realms (SK44). However, it is only through knowledge (jñāna) that one attains freedom from the material process. This knowledge is a special, spiritual knowledge or what we could call "gnosis," that is knowledge that leads to salvation. In the case of Sāṃkhya, gnosis leads to salvation from saṃsāra, the endless cycle of reincarnation.

Gnosis is the central concern of the Indian philosophical schools, because it is the means by which one attains liberation from the painful cycle of death and rebirth. However, the schools interpret differently the content of this special knowledge. For Īśvara, gnosis is the power that is able to distinguish the difference between consciousness and the material world (SK37). In fact, the word "sāṃkhya" means both "discrimination" and "enumeration." Thus the Sāṃkhya School emphasizes that gnosis occurs through correctly discriminating between the fundamental principles of puruṣa and prakṛti. This is achieved by accurately enumerating all the fundamental principles in experience. Contrariwise, it is ignorance of this fundamental duality, which keeps the subtle body bound to the cycle of reincarnation. Thus, the connection between a node of consciousness and the world is real, but the subsequent emergence of the manifest world of experience that then occurs is the result of a mistake or confusion leading to bondage.

Here we encounter a difficulty with Sāṃkhyan dualism. Since the entire world is unconscious, and the buddhi is part of the phenomenal world, how does it attain knowledge? However, since the self is a completely passive witness to the phenomenal world, how can it acquire gnosis, since it doesn't do anything at all? Some contemporary scholars have argued that puruṣa realizes that it is not connected to the material process and thereby attains liberation. However, this goes against the notion in Sāṃkhya that the pure nodes of consciousness are inactive. Other scholars think that it must be the intellect-will that somehow realizes it is not conscious, or that it is not consciousness itself, which leads to liberation. SK62 provides a clue to the solution of this quandary:

Therefore, no one is bound, released, or reborn;
Prakṛti (only) in her various forms is
Reborn, bound, and released.

Here Īśvara implies that the nodes of consciousness are not really bound, but prakṛti "herself" is the one that transmigrates (is reborn again and again).* So what does Īśvara mean when he says that "no one is bound," and that it is prakṛti herself who is bound and released? This refers to the fact that it is only the subtle body that is actually bound to the material process, and not pure consciousness. However, SK55 states,

Here a conscious puruṣa
Suffers decay and death.
Because of the subtle body's continuance,
Suffering occurs through its very nature.

This verse declares that puruṣa suffers because of the existence of the subtle body. As we saw above, the subtle body is connected with the dispositions and it is the dispositions (except for gnosis), which are responsible for continued rebirth in saṃsāra. This is clearly stated in the following two verses:

There is no subtle body without the dispositions;
There are no dispositions without a subtle body.
Thus there arises the twofold creation
Named "subtle body" and "dispositions." (SK52).

---

* In Sāṃkhya prakṛti is metaphorically conceived as female and puruṣa as male (in Sanskrit *prakṛti* is a feminine noun and *puruṣa* is masculine, so the association probably seemed obvious to Indians). This association of Nature as feminine and active, and consciousness as male and passive was to have a long history in Indian thought and influenced the later tantric movements.

But prakṛti alone binds herself with seven forms;
And she alone is released through
One form for the sake of puruṣa (SK63).

Here the obvious interpretation of the "seven forms" and "one form" is that they refer to the eight dispositions. Gnosis would then be the form that releases prakṛti (specifically the subtle body), while the other seven (ignorance, passion, dispassion, virtue, vice, power, and impotence) keep her bound.

Based on what Īśvara is saying in these verses, it must be the buddhi that realizes gnosis. If we are going to assume as the SK states that puruṣas are inactive and always free, then liberation must take place on the side of prakṛti. As manifest prakṛti's first principle, buddhi is the discriminating faculty of the "inner organ" of the subtle body, and is the possessor of the gnosis needed for liberation.

So how do we resolve this with the belief that all of Nature is unconscious? The ancient commentators were also aware of this apparent contradiction and attempted to resolve it with the doctrine of reflection (*pratibimba*). According to this theory, the pure consciousness of puruṣa is reflected in the buddhi like a mirror, which through ignorance believes it is the source of consciousness. In this way, the intellect-will is not conscious in itself, but obtains its awareness through association with a pure node of consciousness (much like the moon receives its light from the sun, but the sun is self-luminous). Another theory sees this reflection as also reflected back toward the node of consciousness (a theory of double reflection), which creates the false impression that puruṣa is somehow involved in the material world (and hence seems to suffer in saṃsāra).

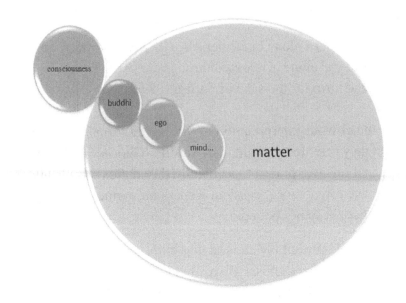

BUDDHI CREATES A CONNECTION BETWEEN CONSCIOUSNESS AND MATTER THROUGH THE POWER OF REFLECTION

So what is the content of this gnosis that allows buddhi to realize the difference between consciousness and matter? The answer comes in one of the most intriguing and enigmatic verses in the *Sāṃkhyakārikā*:

> In this way, through the study of the principles,
> Complete knowledge arises that
> "I am not (this); (this) is not mine; I am not."
> Due to its freedom from error,
> This gnosis is pure and singular. (SK64).

This verse characterizes gnosis as the realization that there is no "I" or "self" to be found anywhere in experience. This means that buddhi realizes that the principle immediately dependent upon it, the ego, generates the rest of the phenomenal world. Thus the intellect-will, through a process of radically dissociating from every phenomenon as "I" or "mine," is able to redirect its attention away from phenomena and realize that its very existence is dependent on pure consciousness as the true source of awareness. In this way, the buddhi through the purity of its sattvic knowledge reflects back the light of pure consciousness toward its source. What happens then?

In SK65, Īśvara tells us that when gnosis is attained puruṣa sees prakṛti (that is witnesses all phenomena as emanating from a single unmanifested source) who, because her purpose has been completed, returns to inactivity. SK66 then states that "And though the connection between them [puruṣa and prakṛti] continues, there is no longer the need for creation." This is because the gnosis attained by buddhi prevents the other dispositions from exerting any continued causal force. Once one attains this realization, the process of karma and rebirth has been stopped, but the body of the sage continues "Through the power of karmic impressions like the spinning of a potter's wheel" (SK67). This means that due to residual karma, the person continues to exist and lives out his/her final life until death. At this point the SK tells us,

> When the body's dissolution has arrived,
> And the originator [prakṛti], her purpose fulfilled, returns,
> Complete and endless isolation is attained. (SK68).

In other words, the intellect-will's knowledge of "not I" and "not mine" means the game is up: the true and ultimate distinction between consciousness and matter has been realized. The Sāṃkhyan sage is now a being who is liberated while still living. Upon the death of the body, the entire phenomenal world returns into a state of perfect equilibrium, while puruṣa remains alone, eternally free and no longer conscious of a phenomenal world.

ON THE PATH TO REALIZATION BUDDHI REDIRECTS ATTENTION INWARD TOWARD THE SOURCE OF CONSCIOUSNESS

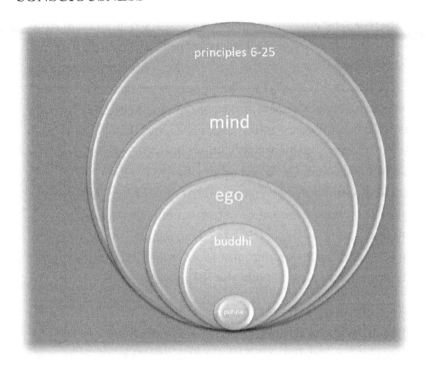

Sāṃkhya and Science

One of the greatest strengths of Sāṃkhya in relation to the contemporary world is its strong compatibility with modern science. Since Sāṃkhya places all of reality (except for pure consciousness) within the natural world of prakṛti, it is not opposed to the naturalistic approach of the sciences. Īśvara is concerned with analyzing the component parts of the phenomenal world according to the guṇas and the principles in order to demonstrate the impersonal and unconscious causal mechanisms underlying the manifest world. However, there is no need to slavishly cling to the doctrines of the guṇas and principles. Instead, we may accept the basic premise of Sāṃkhya, that the world is a vast impersonal causal network, and continue to use the natural sciences of physics, chemistry and biology to better understand it. Likewise, we can use psychology, sociology, anthropology, and the other social sciences and humanities to better understand human beings as part of the social world, which is also located within the natural world of causality. However, the possible sticking point between Sāṃkhya and science is the notion that all sentient life – anything with awareness – exists as a response to pure nodes of consciousness that reside outside of the material world.

Let us now look more closely at the idea that consciousness is separate from matter. A modern materialist might suppose that consciousness is generated by the brain and is actualized in the world as electrochemical changes in the brain's neural network. This has been a working assumption by many scientists and psychologists studying the brain for the last century or so. This we could call the "generation model" of consciousness (that brains generate consciousness). However, there are two possible objections to this. The first we have already mentioned, which is related to the idea that consciousness is "the hard problem" in philosophy of mind. This problem is about the subjective nature of first person accounts of experience. All of our neuroscience and advanced imaging technologies still cannot explain how the neurons firing in my brain leads to my subjective experiences of what the world is like such as the taste of my favorite ice cream, the smell of a rose, or the color red. In other words, there is a gap between the phenomenological experience of the world, or "what it is like" for some subjective consciousness, and our materialist explanations of it.

Now Sāṃkhya claims that the world of matter actually manifests out of a response to consciousness. This view is not unlike the contemporary view that brains actually receive consciousness like radios, rather than generate consciousness from within. On this "receiver model," consciousness is a fundamental property of reality (like gravity or light for example) that exists separate from the material world, and then is connected to it through brains. This view has gained some serious traction in recent years among philosophers and scientists in consciousness studies. The "receiver model" offers a logically coherent alternative to the belief that brains generating consciousness. A strength of the receiver model is that it accepts the insights of the natural sciences, while also recognizing the importance of our subjective experiences of what the world is like (without trying to explain away consciousness). Moreover, it is completely compatible with the Sāṃkhyan view.

Some people might reject in principle the idea of realities existing outside of the material realm. However, in the last few decades modern physics has demonstrated that the world of ordinary matter – that is all atoms, molecules, plants, animals, rocks, planets, stars, galaxies, etc. – only accounts for about 5% of what exists in the universe. Around 27% of the universe is now thought to be made up of "dark matter," and the rest of the universe (about 68%) is believed to be "dark energy." Very little is known about dark matter or dark energy, but suffice to say, we now know that there is a lot more to the universe than simply matter. Thus the Sāṃkhyan view that maintains the separate existence of nodes of consciousness existing apart from the material world is not so implausible after all. Moreover, some popular theories in modern physics (like Superstring Theory) postulate the existence of other dimensions of reality beyond the four of spacetime. One might even be so bold as to speculate that dark matter might be analogous to unmanifest prakṛti and that consciousness could "exist" somehow within "dark energy;" or that consciousness might exist in a different dimension outside of our spacetime continuum.

Another possible issue for a modern person (particularly someone trained in German phenomenology) is the notion that there can be "pure consciousness" outside of someone being conscious of something in particular. Some philosophers would maintain that consciousness is always intentional; in other words, that consciousness is always "conscious of" something. "Pure consciousness," outside of any content, would then make no sense; and talking about such a thing, would be equal to speaking of nothing. Another way of framing this problem is how can we distinguish between pure (contentless) consciousness and nothingness? Insight into this issue can be gained by looking at how Indian philosophers tended to conceptualize consciousness.

A very common metaphor used in Indian philosophy for consciousness is light. In the same way that light is seen as self-luminous (light does not need another source to illuminate itself), consciousness is viewed as being aware of itself. Therefore, pure consciousness (like pure light) would be self-luminous, or conscious that it is consciousness. We see this idea coming to the fore in a common Indian conception concerning "the four states of consciousness." In the first two states of waking and dreaming consciousness, we are aware of objects in experience. In our waking state we perceive objects in the world; in the dream state we perceive dream-objects. In the third state of deep sleep, we don't perceive any objects, but this was not viewed as being unconscious. Since consciousness is "self-luminous" like light, it is still conscious, but not aware of any particular objects, because these have been suppressed by deep sleep. Likewise, "the fourth state" was considered by some such as the Advaita Vedānta School to be beyond the other three and represent pure nondual consciousness as the ultimate ground and nature of reality. Again, this pure consciousness as self-luminous would somehow be aware of itself. One way we could view this is that pure consciousness is the possibility, or pure potential, that consciousness could perceive something outside of itself as an object of awareness; but regardless of whether objects appear, consciousness always remains self-aware of its own existence. This is the Sāṃkhyan view, which differs from Advaita as to the source of the phenomena that appear to consciousness, but nevertheless shares the assumption that consciousness (like light) is self-luminous.

Another possible stumbling block for the contemporary reader of Sāṃkhya might be its ideas about karma and rebirth. Perhaps you don't belief in rebirth or reincarnation. What then would be the point of Sāṃkhya? First, let me say, there is nothing logically incoherent or absurd about the notions of karma and rebirth. Besides the fact that hundreds of millions (if not billions) of people today believe these ideas, there is strong circumstantial evidence of some people (particularly children) at times remembering past lives (see for example, Ian Stevenson's *Twenty Cases Suggestive of Reincarnation*, revised edition, 1988). It is again important to realize that there is nothing irrational or impossible about a belief in reincarnation. However, even if one rejects such notions as "unscientific" or "impossible," I maintain that Sāṃkhya's psychological insights into the nature of suffering and its solution can still be applied to our existential situation in this life, even if this is our "one-and-only" life.

Exercise 6: Observing the Ego

One of the most difficult and subtle principles to observe is the ego, or "I-maker." Most people have no idea that their intellect-will exists separately from their ego. Even in sitting meditation, as you watch your breath and sensations in your body, your ego remains almost invisible to the witnessing consciousness. However, when your feelings are hurt, when your boss yells at you, when you get rejected, when you are frightened, anxious or deeply worried, the contours and structure of the ego come to the fore. These are all opportunities for noticing the "I-maker" in action. Likewise, when you are praised, win an award, get a bonus, etc. those "good" feelings also expose the hidden architecture of the ego.

The next time one of these things happens, stop and notice the part of you observing the "I-maker" as it receives the praise or blame, or undergoes a strong emotional reaction. Notice the gap that exists between the witness and the ego's sense of self. Things that threaten this sense make it feel bad; things that reinforce this self-identity make it feel good. However, the witness just watches and is not affected by any of it.

Be the witness, not the victim of circumstance.

The real power of Sāṃkhya lies in its analysis of our subjective experience of the world, which is occurring right now in this moment-by-moment awareness. In their search for the solution to the problem of suffering, the ancient Sāṃkhyan sages analyzed experience into all of its component parts from the point of view of subjective awareness. Through their analysis they uncovered certain basic phenomenological structures – the intellect, the will, the ego, the mind, the sense organs, the action capacities, the gross material world of fire, water, wind, etc. – that provide the matrix for everything that a person can experience. What the sages could not find in experience was the source of the awareness of the one experiencing, or the source of the phenomena arising within experience. Because every sentient being experiences the world from

43

its own point of view, the ancient sages speculated that there must be many sources of consciousness – one for each being – in order to account for individual differences in perspective.

Another profound insight provided by Sāṃkhya is that our psychological and physiological processes are interlinked and both are part of a closed causal network within the natural world. The presence of consciousness causes the evolution of the manifest world; but other than cause this reaction, puruṣa does not doing anything, but remains a pure witness to experience. As a result the "person" emerges from the interaction of a pure node of consciousness with the Invisible World, resulting in the causal transformations of the three guṇas within experience. Thus, "the person" is like an optical illusion caused by the refraction of the pure light of consciousness upon the buddhi, which consists of an admixture of purity (sattva), impurity (tamas), and activity (rajas).

Sāṃkhya as Psychology

In the beginning of this book, I discuss the idea of "psychologizing" classical Sāṃkhya in order to create what I call "Modern Sāṃkhya," a spiritual path for the contemporary atheist. Hopefully, you have already had some insights in the psychological utility of the system from the ideas we have looked at so far in the main text and the exercises in the textboxes. In this section, I explicitly address the practical psychological application of Sāṃkhya for the modern person. As I mention in the Introduction, some modern commentators see Sāṃkhya as supplying the philosophy, and classical Yoga the practice for a single system based on the duality of puruṣa and prakṛti. I disagree with this view, and think that Sāṃkhya is a complete system unto itself. I maintain this position, because I think for Sāṃkhya the *philosophy is the practice*. By this I mean that through continuous philosophical analysis of experience, students of Sāṃkhya can train themselves to realign their perceptions of the world, and thereby attains freedom from suffering.

The key to Sāṃkhya practice lies in SK64 where Īśvara states, "In this way, through the study of the principles, complete knowledge arises that 'I am not (this); (this) is not mine; I am not'." By analyzing experience according to the principles, one realizes the impersonal nature of the phenomenal world. None of this manifest world belongs to a self; none of it should you identify with as "me" or "mine." However, the modern practitioner need not accept as gospel the 25 principles or the three aspects. The idea behind them, however, is that the natural world functions according to causal laws and it is in a perpetual state of flux and transformation. This is a fundamental insight. Another is that we decide what we identify with or dissociate from in experience through the faculties of our intellect and will. By learning to dissociate from the phenomenal process, we come to realize we are nothing that we can perceive; and yet we exist.

Exercise 7: Letting Mother Nature Drive

Christians have a saying, "Let go, and let God." Daoists aim to "go with the flow" of the Dao, harmonizing with the natural way of events. In Sāṃkhya all of creation manifests for the sake of the liberation of each transcendent subject. In other words, the world is conspiring in your favor. Moreover, most of what you think is "you" is actually part of the natural world: your body, and your mind; even your ego and intellect-will are part of a world of cause and effect, process and change, time and space. We are all interlinked in a causal nexus systemically linked and obedient to the laws of physics, chemistry, biology, etc. Only the puruṣa, the pure witness, resides outside the dimension of time and space, watching the magic dance of prakṛti in all of her wonderful display.

So rather than attempting to control events, to carve out a separate "you" from the world that can manipulate and own things, simply let go, and rest in witness consciousness. Let Mother Nature take the wheel and drive the car of the phenomenal world. Paradoxically, this does not result in apathy or a catatonic state of inactivity. On the contrary, the intellect-will, ego, mind and body begin to harmonize and resonate with the larger causal nexus, whose ultimate meaning and purpose is your liberation.

Like the Buddhist analysis of experience based on the notion of "not-self," Sāṃkhya teaches one to pay attention to the various aspects of subjective experience and not to identify with any of it as "me" or "mine." The main difference between the two is that Sāṃkhya asserts the existence of a witnessing consciousness outside of experience that functions as the subjective center to the experiential world. Buddhism recognizes no such transcendental self. However, if there is no self, who is suffering and who is liberated?

Modern psychology today seems enamored with the practice of Buddhist "mindfulness." As I mention in the Introduction, I too have taught and continue to teach people mindfulness meditation. The etymology of both the Sanskrit (*smṛti*) and Pāli (*sati*) words for mindfulness relates to the idea of recollecting or remembering. In the modern practice of it used by psychologists, this often involves being aware of bodily sensations, the breath, emotions, thoughts, feelings, sounds, etc. in one's immediate environment without judgment or intellectual analysis. This is a type of "bare attention" to what is occurring in the present moment. But notice that such a method involves the same idea as simply witnessing phenomena in a disinterested way. In mindfulness, one does not identify with anything as "me" or "mine," as good or bad, right or wrong. Not grasping at anything and not trying to push anything away are also important principles. In Buddhist thought, this consciousness that is observing everything is considered just another impermanent part of the psychophysical phenomena that appear to consciousness.

Exercise 8: Who is the Witness?

Sit in quiet meditation simply observing whatever phenomena arise and pass away. At any given moment you will be confronted with an array of perceptions, sensations, feelings, thoughts, and emotions. Some are pleasant; some unpleasant. Some are bright and sharp; others are dull and faint. Some perceptions are extremely subtle – a distant bird call, a slight tingling feeling in the toes, a tiny flicker of nostalgia triggered by the hint of a distant memory, and so on.

While watching these phenomena every few breaths, ask yourself the question, "Who is witnessing this?" Search your field of awareness for "the knower of the field," the subject who is aware of the manifest world. Without consciousness, nothing appears. But who is the conscious one?

Take this questioning into your daily activities. When walking down the street, riding the bus, or driving your car, ask, "Who is the witness?" or "Who is experiencing this?" When you feel angry, sad, happy, depressed, joyful, bored, frightened, lonely, amused, annoyed, etc. ask, "Who is feeling this?" When you sprain your ankle, have a headache or backache, catch a cold, orgasm, sneeze, go to the toilet, take a shower, etc. ask, "Who is aware of this?"

The practice of mindfulness is perfectly compatible with the Sāṃkhyan analysis of experience. A practitioner of Sāṃkhya can practice the same techniques of mindfulness with the goal of not identifying with phenomena as "me" or "mine" and by simply observing everything in a disinterested way. Another method is to ask continuously the question, "Who is the witness of all this?" A third method is when meditating to repeat the mantra, "I am the witness," while merely watching and not identifying with whatever arises in awareness. One can practice these techniques in sitting meditation or while going about daily routines. Having a sitting practice definitely helps consolidate one's attention and focus. With seated meditation it is best to have a quiet place you can go to where you will not be interrupted. You can sit for as little as twenty minutes, or for up to an hour. Once or twice a day is good; but find what works best for you.

With continued practice over time, an intuitive knowledge of the witness as pure presence emerges. One begins to intuit source consciousness as a blind-spot at the heart of experience; it is like the presence of an absence; a hole in reality. As the intellect-will becomes more refined with practice, one senses puruṣa as the True Self, an eternally shining Void from beyond spacetime casting its brilliance upon the phenomenal world. As gnosis dawns, phenomena grow brighter and become paradoxically more distinct as one observes them from a more disinterested place. Once one discards ownership of the ego, thoughts, feelings, memories, emotions, beliefs and the body, these appear to recede, merge and morph into the background environment like colors on a painted landscape.

The goal of Sāṃkhya is to eradicate permanently human suffering. This can only happen for the individual and in order to affect it, a radical change of perspective is required. The result of no longer identifying with the psychophysical entity is the end of suffering, the cessation of karma and the isolation of the material process from pure consciousness. However, while the individual's body is still living, life continues until the final passing away of the subtle body at death. How is it, that someone while still alive can be completely free from suffering?

We can understand this from the psychological point of view when we realize that all suffering is the result of some type of identification. Pain does not exist in the abstract. It always belongs to someone. If one no longer associates or identifies with their body or mind, then whether the pain is emotional or physical, it cannot touch the pure witness. Like the watcher of the movie, once you realize you are not the main character in the story, you are no longer affected by what happens to him. This perspective may seem radical to some. Remember that Sāṃkhya philosophers were renouncers –

they had already given up all family ties, social status and material possessions. Dissociating from the psychophysical entity (body-mind complex) is simply renunciation taken to the next level. The end goal was always the transcendence of the cycle of birth and death. The manifestation of the material world herself is only for the release of the pure witness from the process.

However, most modern people do not wish to renounce everything to seek final liberation beyond the rebirth continuum. Many believe such things are religious fantasy. Rather, most modern people from the middle and upper classes seek a spirituality that pays off in terms of more rewarding, more fulfilling lives here and now in this world. They want to be thinner, make more money, have better sex and be in more fulfilling relationships. Basically, they want to be healthier, happier and richer. Some do search for spiritual realization and fulfilment, but very rarely at the cost of renouncing the world and adopting a homeless, celibate lifestyle. So, how can Sāṃkhya help the modern man and woman?

First, let us look at the eight dispositions of the intellect-will. There are four sattvic ones: knowledge, virtue, dispassion, and power; and four tamasic ones: ignorance, vice, passion, and impotence. Although Sāṃkhya is clear that only knowledge (in the form of gnosis that discerns the distinction between puruṣa and prakṛti) leads to ultimate release, the mental training involved in developing that knowledge increases the sattvic qualities of the buddhi. Virtue here means practicing qualities such as nonviolence, honesty, generosity, kindness and compassion. Dispassion is cool level-headedness that does not give in to anger, rage, hate or lust. Power specifically means mental power and mental abilities such as greater clarity of thought, reasoning skills, memory, computing and calculating power. Basically, the sattvic qualities generate good karma, and lead to beneficial results. By gaining more distance from our involvement in the mind-body process, we paradoxically become more effective players in the game of life. The spiritual traditions of India have always viewed this worldly result as a potential danger on the spiritual path. For example, the increased mental powers of the yogin (spiritual aspirant) were traditionally believed to lead to psychic powers. This in turn would create the temptation to use these powers for worldly ends at the detriment of advancement toward liberation.

The practice of Sāṃkhya is about learning to dissociate the transcendent subject from the natural world of causality, change and process. This is difficult because we continuously identify with our bodies and minds, and the actions we believe we perform. However, from the point of view of Sāṃkhya we don't actually do anything – we are merely passive witnesses to the material processes of nature.

One way to develop this new form of awareness is that whenever you are engaged in something think, "I am not doing X." So for example, you are walking down the street, and you think, "I am not walking down the street." You are waiting in line and think, "I am not waiting in line." You can use this with any activity such as, "I am not following my breath," "I am not feeling sad," "I am not feeling tired," "I am not lying down," "I am not planning my evening," "I don't have a headache," etc.

By training this way as often as we can, we naturally begin to rest in the observing consciousness, the transcendent self. Paradoxically, as we become more detached, Nature takes over, completes all tasks and effortlessly gets done what needs doing for us.

But to follow Modern Sāṃkhya doesn't necessarily mean you need to outwardly renounce the world. Remember the goal is a radical change in perspective affected by complete dissociation from the material process. This is done most simply by identifying with the pure disinterested witness. Puruṣa has never been bound by the material process, but simply watches its transformations. In fact the transformations only occur because prakṛti is being watched. Thus for example, as pure consciousness I can happily watch the life and actions of the psychophysical identity named Doug Osto carry on as usual, as I merely observe. Now he is happy; now he is sad; I see him writing a book, raising children, planning a party; in this situation, he is depressed; then he is sick; now he is dying, etc. the story goes on and I am quietly entertained, and perhaps mildly amused by the seriousness of it all. To the extent I am involved, I am subject to suffering; to the extent I am detached, I am free.

Perhaps the medicine seems to you more harmful than the disease. Maybe you are a person who wants to be involved in the dramas and stories that make up a life. You seek the adventure of the ups and downs, and are willing to take the good with the bad. Life includes happiness and suffering; why should one throw out the baby with the bathwater and be so detached from experience that nothing affects her anymore? But here in lies the ultimate beauty of Modern Sāṃkhya – you decide your level of involvement. Perhaps a death in the family, a breakup of a relationship, or a terminal illness is more than you can bear. Then dissociate from it. You are not your body or your mind. You are pure consciousness that transcends the material dimension. Simply allow yourself to observe when you need to, and be as involved and identified as you want to at other times. Use the method as a psychological tool. The worldly benefits from the mental discipline alone are worth the effort. But Sāṃkhya's greatest gift – the power to transcend any hardship – goes far beyond that.

Parting Words

Sāmkhya is not magic. But the methods proposed here will work if applied with diligence. The path I propose is more than self-help; the ancient sages were seeking transcendence, and although I have updated their message for modern ears, I have kept intact the core idea that who we truly are goes beyond the empirical, visible world. Thus this is a spiritual path because it aims at transcendence. Self-help books aim for what I call "better living in saṃsāra." In other words, their highest aspirations are most often this-worldly, or oriented toward the benefits mentioned above – happier, healthier, richer, more fulfilled. Modern Sāṃkhya can help you attain these things, but more as side effects of practice, rather than as its goal. From Sāṃkhya's point of view, such worldly attainments are ultimately of no intrinsic value. No matter how well you play this game, you're still going to get sick, old, and die.

This is a spiritual path for the modern atheist, because it aims at transcendence but without the belief in God, or any supreme being. Īśvara recognizes the reality of the Vedic gods of Hinduism, but considers them nothing more than superhuman beings, subject like we are to the woes of saṃsāra, and incapable of providing any aid in the goal of overcoming suffering. For Sāṃkhya our salvation is up to us. This is not an easy path, and it does not sugar-coat the harsh realities of human suffering in aphorism about the powers of positive thinking. But what it does do is empower us with the knowledge that we have the ability within ourselves to transcend our own finite existence; that we are so much more than this limited psychophysical entity inhabiting a particular point in the spacetime continuum.

Everyone is endowed with their own unique powers and abilities, and therefore, each of us will achieve different results from our efforts. At times progress will be slow, at other times insights will come with ease. But every effort to realize our true, transcendental nature will reap rewards. If you believe in rebirth, rest assured that the full results of these efforts (unlike worldly endeavors) will inevitably come to fruition, if not in this life, then in future lifetimes. If you believe this is it – your one and only life – training to reside in witness consciousness you'll discover reaps its own rewards. Point your aspirations in the right direction and aim high.

Read this text and the translation in the next chapter as often as you like. The exercises are meant to provide basic meditations to begin to internalize the philosophical and psychological insights of the system. Modify your meditations as needed to find what works for you. With time, you will realize that you are your own best teacher. Strive on with diligence!

Exercise 10: I am the Witness

By now the central message of Sāṃkhya should be clear: you are the witness. In other words, you are not your mind or body. You own no possessions, and you have no relationships. You are not a husband, wife, father, mother, brother, sister, daughter, son, boss, worker; you are not white, black, yellow, or red; you have no nationality; you don't have a favorite food; you have no hobbies or addictions; you suffer no illnesses; and have no hopes and dreams. You are beyond all these things. Your true nature resides in a dimension beyond the material realm. Yet again and again, you identify with the body and mind and suffer as a consequence.

The key to training in Sāṃkhya is "mindfulness." To be mindful means to recollect, to remember, to recall. What exactly? That you are merely the witness of experience. As often as you can throughout your day remind yourself, "I am the witness." In this way, when something overwhelming occurs in your life, when the shocking, horrific, terrifying, painful, soul-crushing events take place, or simply when it all gets too much to bear, recall, "I am merely the witness," and feel the power created by this distance. Watch yourself as suddenly you are able to cope, and you do whatever is required of you to get through. And if there is no "getting through," watch calmly as you pass away. Prakṛti knows what to do. The paradox is that the more you let go of a false sense of control and ownership, the more She is able to get the job that needs doing done.

III. Translation of

the *Sāṃkhyakārikā* of Īśvarakṛṣṇa*

Due to the threefold affliction of suffering,
There is the desire to know the means for its removal.
If (some say) this desire is pointless
Since there are perceptual (remedies),
(We say) this is not the case,
Because those (remedies) lack perfection and finality. (1)

Those remedies derived from the Veda
Are like the perceptual ones,
Since they are connected to impurity, destruction and excess.
A superior way, opposite to those, is attained from
Knowing the manifest, the unmanifest and the knower. (2)

Primordial prakṛti is unproduced; the seven (principles),
Beginning with the great one (buddhi), are productive and produced.
But the sixteen are only produced.
Puruṣa is neither productive nor produced. (3)

Since the attainment of knowledge is
From the correct means of knowledge,
Three kinds of correct means are valid:
Perception, inference and reliable authority.

---

* The following is my translation of the Sanskrit text from G. Larson, *Classical Sāṃkhya: An Interpretation of its History and Meaning*, 2nd Revised Edition (Delhi: Motital Banarsidass Publishers, 1979).

This is because all correct means of knowledge are acquired through these three. (4)

Perception is the apprehension of sense objects.
Inference is said to be of three kinds
Associated with the characteristic mark
And the bearer of that mark.
And reliable authority is the word of a respected person. (5)

Inferential proof about perceptual objects
Beyond the senses is attained by analogy.
The invisible, unattainable even by analogy,
Is established through reliable tradition. (6)

(Perception may not be possible because of:)
Distance, proximity, injury to the sense organs,
Mental instability, subtlety, obscuration,
Suppression, or admixture. (7)

Prakṛti is imperceptible due to her subtlety,
Not because she is non-existent.
Her perceptibility is through her effect.
Her effect is the great one and the other principles;
And its form is both the same and different from prakṛti. (8)

The effect is existent (within the cause) because
Nonexistence does not produce anything,
There is the perception of a material cause,
Universal production does not exist,
Production is possible (only) from what is capable of it;
And because of the true nature of causality. (9)

The manifest is caused, impermanent, non-pervasive, active,
Plural, supported, originated, composite, and dependent;

The unmanifest is the opposite of these. (10)

Like the originator (prakṛti), the manifest is
Made of the three guṇas, uniform, objective,
Universal, unconscious, and generative.
Spirit (puruṣa) is the opposite of these. (11)

The guṇas have: the nature of pleasure, pain and lassitude;
The purpose of clarity, activity and restriction;
And the function of mutual subjugation,
Dependency, causation, and conjunction. (12)

Sattva is light and illuminative;
Rajas excites desire and is agitating;
Tamas is heavy and concealing.
And due to their purpose, they function like a lamp. (13)

Non-discrimination, etc. is established
From the nature of the three guṇas,
And because of their nonexistence in their opposite (puruṣa).
Also, the unmanifest (prakṛti) is established,
Due to the nature of the guṇas as cause of the effect. (14)

Due to the measure of divided things, their conjunction,
Their power and function,
The distinction of cause and effect,
And the wholeness of the manifold (world), (15)

The unmanifest is the cause that is made manifest
Through the assemblage of the three guṇas;
And by their transformations like water due to
The special property connected
To each counter-balanced guṇa. (16)

Puruṣa exists because:
The aggregation (of matter) exists for the sake of another;
There is a power that is the opposite of the three guṇas, etc.;
There is an enjoyer of experience;
And because activity is for the sake of isolation. (17)

The plurality of puruṣas is established because of:
The rule (of karma) concerning births, deaths and actions;
Activity not occurring simultaneously;
And because there exists that which is opposite of the three guṇas. (18)

And because of that opposition it is established
Of this puruṣa that it exists as a witness, isolated,
Indifferent, a spectator and inactive. (19)

Due to their connection,
The unconscious subtle body seems as if conscious;
So also does the inactive one (puruṣa) appear active,
Due to the activity of the guṇas. (20)

The connection of the two,
Like a lame man and a blind man,
Is for puruṣa's seeing and for the originator's isolation.
Creation is made from this. (21)

From prakṛti there is the great one;
From that, there is the ego;
From that, there is the group of sixteen;
And from five of that group of sixteen,
There are the five gross elements. (22)

Buddhi is apprehension;
Virtue, gnosis, dispassion, and power

Are its sattvic forms.
Its tamasic forms are the opposite of these. (23)

The ego is self-conceit.
From it a twofold creation emerges:
The group of eleven and the five subtle elements. (24)

From the modified ego is produced the sattvic eleven;
From the tamasic aspect of the originator of elements (ego),
There are the subtle elements;
From the passionate (rajasic) there are both. (25)

The sense faculties are called
Eye, ear, nose, tongue, and skin.
The action faculties are called
Voice, hands, feet, anus, and genitals. (26)

In this manner, the mind has the nature of both;
Because of its identical nature (with the other faculties),
It is the faculty of reflection.
Manifoldness and external differences
Are due to the transformational property of the guṇas. (27)

With regard to sound and the other sense objects,
The function of the five (sense faculties)
Is said to be mere perception;
And of the five (action faculties),
Speaking, grasping, walking, excreting, and orgasm (are their functions). (28)

With regard to their special characteristics,
The three (buddhi, ego, and mind) have dissimilar functions.
The shared function of the inner instrument
Are the five winds beginning with the breath. (29)

It is said that regarding what is perceptible,
The four (buddhi, ego, mind, and a sense faculty) have a function
That is both simultaneous and consecutive.
Likewise, with regard to the imperceptible,
The three (buddhi, ego, and mind) have a former object. (30)

They each undertake their own function,
Which is conditioned by their mutual purpose.
They exist only for the sake of puruṣa.
The instrument is created by nothing else. (31)

The thirteenfold instrument
Seizes, holds, and illuminates its object.
And its tenfold object is
Seized, held and illuminated. (32)

The inner instrument (buddhi, ego, and mind) is threefold.
The outer instrument is tenfold,
And called the "range of the three."
The outer is in the present time;
The inner instrument is in
The three times (past, present, and future). (33)

Of these, the five sense faculties have
Objects that are both specific and nonspecific.
Voice has (only) the object of sound;
But the remaining have five objects. (34)

Since buddhi, with the other inner instruments,
Is absorbed in all objects,
The threefold instrument is the gate-keeper,
And the rest are the gates. (35)

These (instruments), each with their own characteristics,
And special properties derive from the guṇas,
Illuminate the whole world like a lamp,
And present it to buddhi for the sake of puruṣa. (36)

Because of this, buddhi accomplishes
Every enjoyment for puruṣa;
Moreover, buddhi distinguishes the subtle
Difference between the originator and puruṣa. (37)

The subtle elements are nonspecific;
From these five are the five gross elements.
These are taught to be specific,
Tranquil, violent, and stupefied. (38)

The subtle, those born of mother and father,
And the gross elements
Are said to be of three specific kinds.
Of those, the subtle is constant;
Those born of mother and father are subject to rebirth. (39)

The subtle body (liṅga) previously existing,
Independent, constant, bound by the subtle (instruments)
Such as the great one (buddhi), etc.,
Perfumed by the dispositions,
Wanders saṃsāra without enjoyment. (40)

Just as a picture without a canvas,
Or a shadow without a pillar, or such like (to caste it),
So, an unsupported subtle body does not exist
Without specific instruments. (41)

Through its connection to causes and effects,
And from its union with the omnipresent prakṛti,

The subtle body performs like an actor
For the sake of puruṣa. (42)

The innate dispositions,
Both primary and secondary, such as virtue, etc.,
Are perceived to reside in the instrument;
The embryo, etc., reside in its effect. (43)

Through virtue there is movement upward;
Through vice there is movement downward.
It is said through gnosis there is liberation;
But from its opposite (ignorance) there is bondage. (44)

From dispassion there is the dissolution of prakṛti;
From rajasic passion there is saṃsāra;
From power there is non-obstruction;
From the opposite of this, there is the reverse. (45)

This is the intellect's creation, which is classified according to
Misapprehension, incapacity, contentment and accomplishment;
And because of the disturbance caused
By the imbalance of the guṇas,
There are fifty different kinds of it. (46)

There are five kinds of misapprehension;
And due to a defect in the instrument,
Twenty-eight kinds of incapacity.
There are nine types of contentment,
And eight types of accomplishment. (47)

There are eight kinds of tamas and delusion;
There are ten kinds of extreme delusion.
In the same way, there are eighteen forms of darkness
And eighteen forms of complete darkness. (48)

The eleven defects of the faculties together with
The defects of buddhi are said to be incapacity.
The seventeen defects of buddhi are from
Inversions of the (nine) contentments and (eight) accomplishments.
(49)

The nine contentments are conceived as
Four internal called nature, appropriation, time, and fate;
And five external due to the cessation of the object. (50)

The eight accomplishments are examination,
Verbal communication, study,
The threefold destruction of suffering,
Friendship, and generosity.
The previous three kinds are a hindrance to accomplishment. (51)

There is no subtle body without the dispositions;
There are no dispositions without a subtle body.
Thus there arises the twofold creation
Named "subtle body" and "dispositions." (52)

There are eight different kinds of celestial beings,
And five types of animals.
Humans are of one kind.
This in brief is material creation. (53)

Above is an abundance of sattva;
Below, a preponderance of tamas;
In the middle rajas rules;
This is so from Brahmā down to a blade of grass. (54)

Here a conscious puruṣa
Suffers decay and death.

Because of the subtle body's continuance,
Suffering occurs through its very nature. (55)

Thus, prakṛti's effort –
From the great one down to the particular gross elements –
Seems for her own sake,
But is for another;
It is to liberate each puruṣa. (56)

Just as unconscious milk flows
To nourish a calf,
So the originator functions
To liberate puruṣa. (57)

Just as a worldling performs actions
To satisfy his desires,
So the unmanifest acts
To liberate puruṣa. (58)

Just as a dancer stops her dance
Once viewed by the audience,
So prakṛti disappears once she
Displays herself to puruṣa. (59)

In various ways, she is a helper
To spirit who is no help;
Possessed of the guṇas she acts selflessly
For him who is without guṇas. (60)

I believe there is nothing more delicate than prakṛti,
Who thinks, "I have been seen,"
And never again appears before puruṣa. (61)

Therefore, no one is bound, released, or reborn;

Prakṛti (only) in her various forms is
Reborn, bound, and released. (62)

But prakṛti alone binds herself with seven forms;
And she alone is released through
One form for the sake of puruṣa. (63)

In this way, through the study of the principles,
Complete knowledge arises that
"I am not (this); (this) is not mine; I am not."
Due to its freedom from error,
This gnosis is pure and singular. (64)

Thus, puruṣa, abiding within himself like a spectator,
Sees prakṛti, freed from her seven forms;
And since her aim is achieved,
She returns to her origin. (65)

The indifferent one thinks, "I see her,"
And the other, realizing, "I have been seen," stops.
And though the connection between them continues,
There is no longer the need for creation. (66)

Once the causal force of virtue, etc. has been ended
By achieving true gnosis, the existing body continues
Through the power of karmic impressions
Like the spinning of a potter's wheel. (67)

When the body's dissolution has arrived,
And the originator, her purpose fulfilled, returns,
Complete and endless isolation is attained. (68)

The supreme sage has proclaimed
This secret gnosis about puruṣa,

Wherein he reflects upon the
Existence, birth and destruction of all beings. (69)

Out of compassion, the sage bestowed
This most pure teaching upon Āsuri;
And Āsuri gave it to Pañcaśikha,
Who expanded the system. (70)

This doctrine was passed down through a succession of disciples,
And then thoroughly learned by the noble Īśvarakṛṣṇa,
Who abbreviated it in ārya meter. (71)

Indeed, every topic of the complete *Ṣaṣṭitantra*
Is in these seventy verses,
Except for the short stories,
And arguments of opponents. (72)

Therefore, this condensed treatise
Is not deficient in its sense;
And is like a mirror image reflecting
The vast body of the system. (73)

Made in the USA
Monee, IL
12 March 2020